POCKETGUIDE SERIES

W9-CCH-151

A Proactive Law Enforcement Guide for the War on Terror

LOU SAVELLI

Looseleaf
Law Publications, Inc.

43-08 162nd Street • Flushing, NY 11358
www.LooseleafLaw.com • 800-647-5547

ISBN 1-889031-98-4

This publication is not intended to replace, nor be a substitute for, any official procedural material issued by your agency of employment or other official source. Looseleaf Law Publications, Inc., the author and any associated advisors have made all possible efforts to ensure the accuracy and thoroughness of the information provided herein but accept no liability whatsoever for injury, legal action or other adverse results following the application or adoption of the information contained in this book.

Cover design by *Sans Serif, Inc.* Saline, Michigan

About the Pocketguide Series

Law Enforcement Officers (LEOs) are faced with ever-changing trends and issues and have little time to spend on in-depth research and reference. The Pocketguide series of books has been created to assist law enforcement officers in the endeavor to remain up-to-date on these ever-changing trends. The Pocketguide series provides *to the point* reference information on contemporary important issues.

We at CTS Associates Incorporated, creators of the Pocketguide series, have painstakingly researched and developed the following valuable and useful information.

The Pocketguide books, as you will see, will provide a current, quick and easy-to-use, pocket-sized tool that was written in an easy to read style. When hundreds of pages of information or volumes of material are not feasible to carry around and time does not permit its study, the Pocketguide books will fill that void and provide the right reference.

Please enjoy this useful pocket-sized book and keep in mind that we at CTS Associates Incorporated wish you safety and efficiency in your endeavor to fight the scourge of crime in our society.

Other Pocketguides now available:

Identity Theft
Basic Crime Scene Investigation
Gangs and Their Symbols

Call Toll-Free for other Recent Editions to the
Pocketguide Series and a *Free* catalog.

(800) 647-5547
Looseleaf Law Publications, Inc.
Flushing, NY

About the Author

Lou Savelli, is a 23-year veteran of law enforcement. He has spent his last 21 years with the NYPD and has conducted countless criminal investigations as a proactive plainclothes street cop, a detective, and a detective squad commander. He boasts that he has spent his entire career on the streets in pursuit of criminals and fighting crime because he loves it. He says he learned more about crime-fighting from the criminals on the streets than he did from any Police Academy he attended.

While he has spent many years, in his off-duty time, working toward a continuing education at John Jay College of Criminal Justice and the State University of New York, he feels the education he received from the streets of New York City, the men and women of the NYPD, the other agencies he has worked alongside, the great bosses he has worked under, and the street smarts he has gained, enabled him to survive and thrive as a crime fighter.

Twice awarded 'Supervisor of the Year,' he was recognized by then Police Commissioner William Bratton as one of NYPD's most effective leaders of all ranks (out of 10,000 supervisors) and the NYPD's first supervisor highlighted in the Leadership Newsletter for his outstanding leadership role in his highly successful Anti-Crime Unit.

In 1996, Lou Savelli created and commanded NYPD's first street gang unit called CAGE (Citywide Anti-Gang

Enforcement Unit), which was awarded the National Gang Crime Research Center's award for The Most Effective Gang Unit in the United States. Since then, several gang units across the US and Canada have modeled themselves after the proactive methods used by the CAGE Unit.

Lou Savelli is the Vice President, and cofounder, of the East Coast Gang Investigators Association and one of the original members of the International Counter Terrorism Officers' Association. He has been a career-long member of dozens of other law enforcement associations but credits the Police Writers' Association with encouraging him to write. Lou Savelli has not only been a player in the game of fighting crime, on duty and off, but says he is also a student of it. He said, *"When you think you know all there is about catching criminals and preventing crime, you probably will get shot by a perp that day! There is always more to learn!"* According to Lou, the best advice he ever received was from his father, deceased since 1979, when he said: *"Always keep seeking knowledge because when you stop learning, you're dead!"*

Lou Savelli, who has authored numerous other law enforcement books, written several published short stories, and numerous articles, is also the Vice President in charge of Operations for CTS Associates Incorporated, a Law Enforcement Consulting and Training company.

As a Detective Squad Commander of the NYPD's Terrorism Interdiction Unit, formed as a result of 9-11-01, and a veteran of Ground Zero, Lou Savelli believes that the only way to fight terror is to be proactive and aggressive. He says there is an imminent threat from terrorist cells within the borders of the United States and all law enforcement officers must take a proactive role in hunting down terrorists in every city in America.

Dedication & Remembrance

Please remember the sacrifices made by the men and women of American Law Enforcement, Firefighting Agencies and Emergency Medical Services on September 11, 2001. They are our heroes!

NYPD
FDNY
FBI
FDNY-EMS
FDNY-Fire Marshals
PAPD
NY State Court Officers
NY State Tax Enforcement
Secret Service
US Fish and Wildlife Service

Remember all the victims of the September 11 attacks and other terrorist attacks against America and Americans. Please remember our Armed Forces who have died and support those who are protecting the American Way!

Table of Contents

Introduction

This *Proactive Law Enforcement Guide for the War on Terror* was created to be a handy pocket reference and procedural guide to be utilized in the war on terrorism within the homeland. It is intended to be useful to any law enforcement officer who wants to become involved in the pursuit of terrorists and the security of their communities. This Pocketguide is not intended to replace departmental procedures or local laws pertaining to terrorism or related issues.

This Pocketguide, can be used by many law enforcement officers. It will show how they can become valuable soldiers in the fight against terrorism. This Pocketguide can be useful to:

- ✓ Police Officers
- ✓ Detectives
- ✓ Supervisors
- ✓ Narcotics Agents
- ✓ Tactical Officers
- ✓ Vice Investigators
- ✓ Military Forces

- ✓ Corrections Officers
- ✓ Parole Officers
- ✓ Probation Officers
- ✓ Highway Patrol
- ✓ Federal Agents
- ✓ Military Police
- ✓ Investigators

The information, definitions, techniques and methods detailed in this Pocketguide have been compiled from a variety of trusted sources. The information, definitions, techniques and methods are merely suggestions and reminders to maintain an organized and efficient manner of deployment, investigation and interdiction as it relates to uncovering and thwarting terrorists. At no time do the writers and researchers of this work claim that it should replace officer safety procedures, departmental procedures or official guidelines. Additionally, the legal guidelines existing in each jurisdiction must prevail for the legality of one's actions and the admissibility of resulting information, arrests or evidence. Throughout this book, words will be outlined indicating there is a definition at the end of the book in the Glossary of Terms and Definitions.

This war on terror is a new war that must be fought on several fronts. Since September 11, 2001, law enforcement officers everywhere must take a proactive role to identify terrorists and their supporters as well as relentlessly applying pressure to criminal activity used by terrorists to sustain their evil operations. Terrorists, such as (executed) Tim McVeigh, and (wanted dead or alive) Osama bin Laden, along with their supporters, are a threat to the freedom we all enjoy. The only true fight against terrorism is a fight from all sides. Law enforcement efforts and military operations will win the fight against terror. This *Proactive Law Enforcement Guide for the War on Terror* will help law enforcement efforts in that endeavor.

Threats to America

On February 23, 1998, Osama bin Laden issued a **fatwa,** which is a religious ruling in the religion of Islam, stating in part: "…with God's help – call on every **Muslim** who believes in God and wishes to be rewarded to comply with God's order to kill Americans and plunder their money wherever and whenever they find it!"

On August 28, 1998, from a prison cell in New York City, Muslim cleric, Sheikh Omar Mohammad Abdel Rahman issues a fatwa: *"...Spoil their trade, burn their companies, drown their boats and target their planes and kill the Americans on the land, in the oceans and in the air...Allah will help you against them!"*

In a Statement by the late William Pierce (aka Andrew Macdonald), founder of the National Alliance and author of the racist cult book, *The Turner Diaries*, he said: ***"One day, there will be real, organized terrorism - aimed at bringing down the (US) government!"***

Law Enforcement's War on Terror

The events of September 11, 2001, have forcibly shown us how widespread terrorism can become. It also showed us there is no place safe from an attack. Whether you live or work in a major city or rural town, the threat of terrorism is ever present. While the distance between rural Shanksville, Pennsylvania and metropolitan Washington, DC is only 400 miles, the fabrics of these two American communities are quite different. One is a bustling metropolis and the other is quiet scenic sprawl. I am sure that the thought of a terrorist strike was the furthest thing from the minds of the citizens of both communities. And consider the differences and distance between Oklahoma City, which suffered an attack from the work of a homegrown terrorist, Timothy McVeigh, and New York City. What did these four communities have in common? I think the answer is simple: American Freedom!

To put a stop to terrorism, American law enforcement must take a major role in the effort. Understanding where the threats may be coming from and committing to interdiction is the responsibility of every law enforcement officer in America. And when law enforcement officers exceed 600,000 there is no greater force in the world prepared for this fight! This guide will illustrate what the greatest law enforcement resources in the world can do to stop terror in its tracks. The commitment to fight terrorists within the borders of these United States should be fought aggressively, in the memory of every law enforcement

The World Trade Center
1 day after the attack

officer and each innocent victim that died during an act of terrorism, whether it was April 19, 1995 (Oklahoma City) or September 11, 2001.

Never Surrender to Terrorism! and Never, Ever, Forget!

Understanding Terrorists:
Foreign and Domestic

While foreign and domestic terrorists are different, they have several traits that make them very similar. Foreign and domestic terrorists share similar ideology. This ideology usually materializes in anti-American sentiment. They believe that America is evil and oppressive. Sometimes, America is referred to as the devil, or Satan. This ideology can also be displayed in anti-Semitic doctrine. Anti-Semitic diatribes are usually abundant. Jews are referred to as Zionist bloodsuckers and the United States government is called **ZOG** (Zionist Occupied Government). When the World Trade Center in New York City was attacked on September 11, foreign terrorists such as Islamic Radicals and their domestic counterparts, such as the neo-Nazis, celebrated the death and destruction in, as they say, "*Jew York"* and applauded the killing of many Jewish victims and representatives of the US government (police and fire-fighters).

Foreign and Domestic Terrorists have also shown total disregard for civilian casualties. The al-Qaeda suicide pilots didn't care that the four hijacked airliners were filled with non-government passengers just like Timothy McVeigh did not care that the **Edward P. Murrah Building** also housed a child day care center. Their sordid beliefs refer to that as '*collateral damage.*' If this is truly war, or jihad, why do these cowards carry out their missions against soft targets filled with defenseless civilians? Undoubtedly, cowardice is another shared trait!

Innocent victims of the **Aum Shinrikyo**
Terrorist Attack in Japan

Another common trait is the utilization of crime. Crime is a common way to finance terrorist operations. Many terrorists commit crimes, such as weapons dealing and drug smuggling, to raise money for the purchase of explosives, **weapons of mass destruction,** or financing of everyday operations. A variety of other crimes are becoming popular among terrorists and their supporters to raise money for the funding of operations. Crimes, such as fraud, have become more common among terrorists. Fraudulent identification items such as drivers' licenses, identification cards, social security cards, and passports, have been frequently discovered on terrorists.

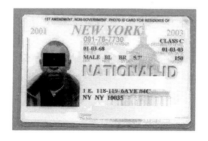

While more about crime will be discussed later in this book, it is important to understand that terrorists often believe their criminal activity is authorized by a higher authority and thus, is standard operating procedure.

Synergy Can Win the War Against Terror

Until recently, there was little coordination and cooperation between law enforcement agencies when it came to terrorist investigations. Antiquated protocol and bureaucratic dinosaurs hindered the ability of law enforcement to work together. Now, federal law enforcement agencies such as the FBI and CIA, which are at the forefront of the effort against terrorism, are sharing information and resources with local agencies.

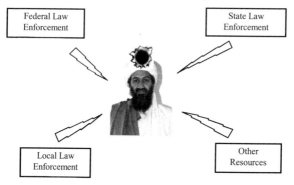

This coordinated effort between the many existing, newly created, and expanded, terrorist task forces and the countless local law enforcement agencies, is the greatest tool against terrorism in our lifetime. This coordinated effort of all the agencies, federal, state, and local, operating toward the same goal, will create greater results than in the past. This is called **synergy**. Synergistically, we will win the war against terrorism.

Information: *It's a Two-Way Street!*

Information is an important weapon against terrorism. In this great nation, there is a variety of ways to acquire information. Without information, tracking terrorists and terrorist cells will be extremely difficult. It is my guess that someone in America had information about the attacks of September 11, 2001, before they happened. Aggressively acquiring information and appropriately disseminating information to the proper law enforcement officials will greatly enhance anti-terror efforts. This information flow, however, must be a two-way street.

There are three simple rules to follow regarding information. These rules are:

1. *Acquisition*
2. *Analysis*
3. *Dissemination*

It is every law enforcement officer's responsibility to follow these three rules in totality. Information can be acquired at a variety of places from a variety of people.

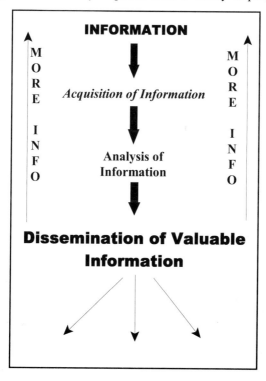

Many people do not realize they have information useful to the efforts against terrorism. Law enforcement officers are experts at acquiring information from people. Analyzing the acquired information is a bit more difficult. Knowing what is useful and what isn't may be a tough task but it is an important one. Information must be carefully analyzed before it is dismissed or discarded. Intelligence databases and law enforcement officers' minds and notepads are filled with information left unanalyzed. This information could be the key to uncovering a sleeper cell or another terrorist attack. More importantly, information is a two-way street. What comes in, must go out. Sharing information, unless the information is absolutely confidential, is imperative! In the past, too much information was not shared. Today, there is no time for not sharing information.

I always say, *"Knowledge is power and information is the tool to obtain that power!"* Giving knowledge to the masses in law enforcement, by those who have the knowledge, empowers the masses to accomplish great things. Information disseminated to the nearly 1 million law enforcement officers nationwide, in essence, renders them a massive counter-terrorism team. This will result in the capture of terrorists, the thwarting of planned acts, and the acquisition of an abundance of useful information.

Fighting Crime: One Step Beyond!

When is comes to terrorism, just fighting crime is not enough. We must go beyond the norm. Understanding that terrorist organizations commit crimes as a means to achieve their goals, law enforcement officers must be ever alert. Consider the following questions when coming in contact with crime and criminals:

- Could this crime be part of a terrorist plot?
- Could it finance terror?
- Do the perpetrator's traits or statements indicate a terrorist profile?
- Did the crime committed take multiple perpetrators?
- Does this crime earn the perpetrators an exorbitant amount of money?
- Is this money traceable?

Conventional crime fighting techniques and investigative tactics need to be enhanced by more thorough efforts. The time for the relentless pursuit of crime and criminals, and the aggressive enforcement of laws, is now! Serious felonies and petty offenses must be attacked with the same zeal. One never knows where the tidbit of information may surface that can uncover a terrorist plot or cache of explosives. Who knows whom the next informant may be that can provide this information. Be assured, fighting crime beyond the normal effort will increase the odds.

Be Aware of Terrorist Indicators

Law Enforcement officers should be aware of terrorist indicators. Awareness of these indicators will give the law enforcement officer a strong basis to recognize terrorist related information upon being exposed to it. Such indicators are: negative rhetoric, inflammatory statements, suspicious situations, surveillance, excessive physical training, anti-American literature or a disregard for US laws.

Terrorists and their supporters tend to act similar since many of them have trained in the same terrorist training camps and share the same negative ideology. Foreign terrorists and their supporters, such as **Islamic radicals**, trained in camps designed by **Osama bin Laden**. Many of these Islamic radicals and their supporters follow the guidelines of the **al-Qaeda Manual** which sets forth operating procedures for members of terrorist cells.

Rough translation from an Arabic dialect:
"....cure the cancer!"

This graffiti was photographed in a neighborhood known to have terrorists and terrorist supporters living within its boundaries. It was photographed in August 2001 in New York City.

17

Even domestic terrorists will give some indications, at some point, of their ideology or share the same indicators as their foreign partners. Such terrorist indicators are:

- ✓ Possession of fake or altered identification
- ✓ IDs from different states
- ✓ Possession of IDs or passports in which the person looks dramatically different in each photo
- ✓ Possession of anti-American, anti-Jewish, anti-minority, or anti-Israel material such as an upside down American Flag or inflammatory literature
- ✓ Possession or use of disrespectful writing or graffiti regarding America, Jews, minorities, or Israel
- ✓ Lived in several states in the past few years
- ✓ Taken multiple trips out of the country or state of residence in the past few years
- ✓ Multiple identification in different names
- ✓ Possession of videos, photos or diagrams of public buildings, airports, subways, malls, etc.
- ✓ Conducting surveillance of government employees and government sites
- ✓ Taken flying lessons or use of flight simulators
- ✓ Extreme interest in Martial Arts and aggressive fighting techniques
- ✓ Use of internet cafes, library internet access and computer store with internet capability to avoid tracing

- ✓ Use of payphones and phone cards rather than his/her own phone
- ✓ Possession of large amounts of money or evidence of an overseas transfer of money (money transactions of under $10 thousand are done to avoid filing a **CTR**)
- ✓ Receiving large amounts of money from overseas
- ✓ Renting first floor apartments to facilitate an easy escape
- ✓ Extended use of inexpensive motels since there are not usually any surveillance cameras
- ✓ Never allowing maids to clean the room alone or the person is always in attendance while the maid is working
- ✓ No apparent means of legitimate income
- ✓ Member of a radical organization
- ✓ Display of terrorist/**extremist** symbols
- ✓ Recent shaving of head and body hair: Indication of suicide bomber *"Purification Process"*

Common Crimes Associated
With Terrorists

Terrorists and terrorist support organizations will most likely be involved in crime. The basic reason for the crime is to obtain funding or supplies for the organization to sustain itself or to carry out terrorist acts. Many terrorists engage in crimes such as international drug smuggling and domestic drug trafficking as well as weapons trafficking. In the case of foreign terrorists operating in the United States, their crimes, generally, are low risk with high profits. These crimes will minimize contact with law enforcement but maximize the potential for making a lot of money. Such crimes, like those mentioned in the following pages, are seldom fully investigated and considered a low-priority for law enforcement. In the majority of cases, a fine is charged in lieu of a jail sentence. The money trail is seldom investigated and the link to terrorism overlooked. The offenders are free to continue to victimize the American consumer, profits continue to mount and the results are exorbitant amounts of American money to fund terrorist acts against America and other western countries.

Mail Theft

An example of such crimes is the theft of credit cards and checks from the mail. On a good day, especially in a suburban or rural setting where the mailboxes are externally situated, dozens of credit cards and government checks can be easily stolen. Terrorists and terrorist support groups can sell a stolen credit card for as much as $500 each while they can get as much as 25% of the value of the stolen check. These crimes are more prevalent on the first few days of each month because the government checks are mailed on the last day of each month. The victims of these crimes are the intended recipient of the checks or credit cards and the issuing entity. These crimes are doubly attractive to terrorists because, in their minds, they consider *(in their own twisted way)* their victims to be the US government and the Jews who run the government and the banks and not the people who receive the mail. This makes the crime justified.

Investigation Methods

Many times, a victim of mail theft never reports the incident because they never know it actually happened. There is seldom a witness. The victim, realizing they have not received their check or a new credit card in the mail, usually contacts the government agency or credit card company to issue a new check or credit card. These crimes are seldom reflected on local crime complaint statistics and the local law enforcement agencies do not give it much attention. To determine if such a crime is happening in your area, contact the local Postal Inspectors office. They will be able to inform you where and when the crimes are happening. A local (official or unofficial) task force should be created to identify and investigate these crimes. Other methods of investigation of mail theft is the utilization of informants, aggressive interdiction against such fencing operations and networking with Treasury Agents and Credit Card investigators to locate the persons involved, the areas where these crimes are occurring and how they are cashing the checks or using the credit cards.

Coupon Fraud

Coupon fraud is another lucrative crime committed by terrorists and terrorist support organizations. According to expert testimony before the 1998 Congressional Hearings on Intelligence and Security, more than $150 million, annually, in coupon related fraud proceeds are diverted to fund terrorism.

Usually, someone affiliated with the terrorist organization, or a terrorist cell itself, owns or works at a local convenience store or supermarket. From this store, or its clandestine coupon cutting/sorting houses, coupons obtained from magazines, circulars and newspapers will be cut, sorted and placed in piles. The coupons are sorted and stacked according to the product and sent to a certified Retail Coupon Clearinghouse to which the main store is a registered customer. The Retail Coupon Clearinghouse issues a rebate check to the registered store in the amount of the coupons received. These rebate checks will value in excess of hundreds, and many times, thousands of dollars. This process is repeated every month. While few or none of the actual items have been sold by the store, the company will issue this check without investigating. Most of the time, the companies and manufacturers do not prosecute those caught committing the fraud. Frequently, this type of crime is committed by dozens of stores within the same terrorist network at the same time.

Obviously, if done carefully and by many persons, the coupon cutters can make incredible amounts of money for the terrorist organization. This coupon fraud scenario was used by the Palestine Liberation Front, Abu Nidal Organization and Sheik Abdel Rahman's **Jihad** Organization, responsible for the 1993 World Trade Center bombing which killed 6 people and injured 1,000.

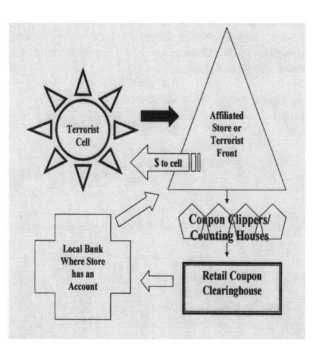

Terrorist Cell

Affiliated Store or Terrorist Front

$ to cell

Coupon Clippers/ Counting Houses

Local Bank Where Store has an Account

Retail Coupon Clearinghouse

Investigation Methods

Coupon fraud investigation is extremely difficult. The law enforcement officer interested in such crimes should contact the **Association of Certified Fraud Examiners** *at www.cfenet.com/about/about.asp*.

Cigarettes and Related Crimes

Another lucrative crime is the sale of untaxed cigarettes. In states like New York and California, cigarettes are sold for high prices because of high, imposed, taxes. A carton of cigarettes, in some states, can be purchased duty-free for as little as $14.50 per carton, while in other states, a carton will sell for as much as $44.50 per carton. When cigarettes are illegally smuggled into states at a price of $14.50 to $20 per carton and sold at the (legal) price of $44.50 per carton that results in profits as high as $30 per carton. Many Islamic terrorists and support cells, as well as American terrorist extremists and organized crime, are heavily involved in this type of crime because of the profits and lack of law enforcement attention. Many, when discovered or arrested, usually receive a fine or probation. This crime will become more prevalent because of the increase in taxes on cigarettes across the country.

In New York City, wholesale cigarette prices were raised (8/2002) to $28.00 per carton. The tax imposed on a carton of cigarettes in New York City is $31.00 per carton. Retailers are selling a carton of cigarettes in NYC for $75.00 per carton in order to make a profit. That will result in smokers paying up to $7.50 per pack of cigarettes.

Tax Stamp is affixed to
the bottom of each Pack

Taking it one step further, Islamic Terrorists, and their supporters, commonly counterfeit state cigarette tax stamps, affix them to packs of cigarettes, thus avoiding detection of untaxed and out-of-state cigarettes. This also saves them $31.00 in taxes per carton of cigarettes. While many of these counterfeit tax stamps are illegally printed in the USA, some counterfeit tax stamps seized have been printed in places like Egypt and Yemen. The crimes violated during the typical illegal cigarette operation run by terrorists are Tax Evasion, Forgery and Interstate Transportation to Avoid Taxation.

Investigation Methods

Cigarette enforcement and investigation is quite simple, the majority of cigarette crimes are committed in stores that involve the sale of cigarettes to the average retail customer in order to make a profit. One method is to cultivate the help of a local merchant involved in the sale of cigarettes to the public. Ask them to contact you if they are approached by salesmen of counterfeit or untaxed cigarettes. Another method is the inspection of less than reputable stores selling cigarettes. In most states, a license must be obtained to sell these cigarettes and collect taxes. Your local taxation investigators should have the authority to conduct inspections of such merchants.

The Baby Formula Scam

There are several variations of the Baby Formula Scam being perpetrated by terrorists and terrorist funding outfits. These scams are difficult to identify and more difficult to prosecute. There are four types of the scam:

Counterfeit Formula: The counterfeiters (terrorist cells or supporters) will counterfeit liquid and powdered forms of baby formula and sell it to local stores at a discounted price well below the real product. While some store owners are not aware that the baby formula is counterfeit, other store owners are aware of the counterfeit formula and just want to reap larger profits. There are, however, stores involved with the counterfeiters and terrorist organizations that are part of the baby formula conspiracy.

Good/Bad Mix: In the good/bad mix, the perpetrators will purchase large amounts of baby formula (canned) and mix the lot with expired or counterfeit or cans of baby formula that cost them near to nothing to acquire. Often enough, counterfeit labels with new expiration dates are affixed to the expired cans of baby formula. Some cans, after removing the labels, may be punctured to draw out good formula and fill up with old or counterfeit formula to increase the amount of total formula cans. The holes in the can are covered with glue and hidden under the old label or a counterfeit label.

Expired Formula: The perpetrators of this scam will purchase, steal or take from the garbage of large retailers, wholesalers and manufacturers, expired or damaged cans of baby formula. The cans of baby formula are acquired for pennies. They will affix a counterfeit label with a new expiration date.

Formula Theft: In this scam, local criminals and gang members are employed to shoplift cans of baby formula and will be paid a dollar or more for every can they can steal. The baby formula fence or store (possibly terrorist owned) will sell each can at the regular price.

Consider the profits of the sale of baby formula when the terrorist or their supporters are paying next to nothing. Also, consider the unsuspecting parents feeding their children counterfeit, unsanitary, expired or other unhealthy forms of baby formula. What if a child is lactose intolerant and fed an alleged soy product that is really a lactose product mislabeled with a counterfeit label?

Investigation Methods

A good start in the investigation process against baby formula scams is to familiarize all law enforcement officers, through training, with legitimate baby formula products and their features. Thereafter, contacting local merchants and employing their help against such scams and illegal peddlers of baby formula. Periodic inspections of stores may result in the identification of such scams and their perpetrators.

Identity Theft

A fast-growing crime, especially between terrorist funding and terrorist ID document circles, is **Identity Theft**. Identity theft is a profitable business for terrorists and a way for them to acquire valid identification documents in someone else's name. First, let's discuss the way Identity Theft is perpetrated. The identity thief obtains specific information about an individual in the form of a date of birth, social security number, or credit card number. This theft of identity information is usually perpetrated through an unscrupulous store clerk selling identity information from credit applications, criminals sifting through personal trash or banks for the information, and elaborate internet scams designed to get people to divulge their information.

The identity criminal, especially in the case of terrorists, will create a new address and reroute new credit cards to be delivered to the address. A checking account(s) will be opened in the name of the stolen identity. In a short period of time, generally before the next monthly statement is sent to the victim, credit cards are charged to the maximum; many goods are ordered and delivered to a **drop address** where the criminal or an accomplice takes possession of the goods. Checks are written in high amounts and cashed before the recipients find out there are insufficient funds in the accounts.

The new identity, created on the original information, can be used to board planes, travel in and out of the country and a host of other activities where ID documents are needed. At the end of the time that the identity criminal has abandoned the use of the identity, many crimes have been committed, much money has been made, the victim has a destroyed credit history and the criminal is on to another identity crime as easy as the previous one.

Terrorists have been caught with someone else's identity information, either in the form of a laundry list on a piece of paper with the information (date of birth, social security number, credit card number) or credit cards and checks in someone else's name. Law enforcement officers must be cognizant of this when searching suspects and encountering suspected terrorists.

Investigation Methods

Identity theft is usually discovered by the victim of the crime. The victim will report it to police. The police will conduct an investigation that is extremely difficult to succeed. To investigate identity theft, especially when it comes to terrorists, law enforcement officers must become aggressive. Complaints of identity theft should be reviewed for patterns, and all officers should be trained on how to identify identity theft and identity theft criminals. Unscru-

pulous store clerks, when discovered, should be arrested and prosecuted to develop information on criminals buying identity information and perpetrating identity theft.

The Credit Card Bust Out Scam

Credit card bust out scams are extremely popular between terrorist funding operations, terrorist money laundering operations, and **Middle Eastern Organized Crime (MEOC)**. Credit cards are obtained from individuals leaving the country who hand over their credit card(s) to a credit card bust out scam artist. The scam artist runs up the credit card's credit line to its limit. The scam artist will sometimes pay the credit card quickly to raise the limit on the card. Once the cash and goods obtained reaches the largest monetary amount possible, the credit card scam artist notifies the person who handed over the card (cardholder) to report the card stolen. The cardholder receives ten to thirty percent of the profit. The cardholder is never penalized nor responsible for the charges since the credit card was reported stolen and he/she was out of the country.

Credit card bust out scams are difficult to enforce. Law enforcement officers should educate community merchants and department stores on this scam. Merchants should be asked to request other pieces of identification with photos affixed when accepting credit cards. Law enforcement officers should be alert to individuals in possession of someone else's credit cards.

Assumed Name Credit/Identity

Many terrorists assume the identity of persons who have left the country or been deported by the US government. Most of the time, the perpetrator of these crimes knows the person who has left the country or been deported. The terrorist or illegal alien assumes the identity of the person who left the country, reaps great profits from the financial accounts, and is able to travel about the US with a new identity.

Investigation Methods

Alert law enforcement officers, informants, and business owners are the best investigation method against this crime. When approaching suspected terrorists, multiple forms of identification, especially those with photos, should be produced. Computer checks will reveal information that a perpetrator may not know about the real person.

Forged/Counterfeit Checks/Money Orders

Because of the exorbitant amounts of money that can be obtained from forged or counterfeit checks and money orders, many terrorist groups, and organized crime, are engaging in, or more frequently, becoming involved. Most banks or stores cashing checks may not find out the check or money order is a forgery, or counterfeit, until several days later. Places cashing these checks or money orders seldom ascertain if the account has sufficient funds, if any, in the account. The perpetrator only shows identification, usually forged or obtained from Identity Theft, and poses as the person cashing the check or money order.

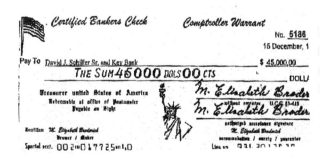

Investigation Methods

In order to investigate forged checks or money orders, a law enforcement officer should familiarize himself with common security features on most checks and money orders today. These features include a watermark, bleeding logos and print (runs with moisture), coordinated check serial numbers and last digits on account, financial institution information and microscopic print. For more information, and to become involved in the investigation of such crimes, contact the National Check Fraud Bureau.

EBT/USDA Swipe Card Fraud

Since the crime of stolen and counterfeit food stamps and welfare fraud became so popular and an enormous moneymaker for terrorists, organized crime, common thieves and benefit recipients intent on defrauding the government, the Electronic Benefits Transfer (EBT) was created. The EBT is a credit card issued by the state of residency and the US Department of Agriculture that the recipient can use to obtain money and benefits pursuant to disbursed government benefits. There is an electronic record of what was purchased, where it was purchased and when it was purchased. Instead of food stamps, the benefits recipient uses the card at an ATM machine (if the benefit account allows), pharmacy or grocery store to obtain necessary goods and services.

Of course, every foolproof idea is compromised by those with criminal intent. Many terrorist organizations own or are involved with employees of stores accepting the EBT cards and this is where the crimes happen. Store clerks swipe the cards for a monetary amount of goods for a customer (benefit recipient) using the EBT who wishes to obtain cash instead of goods. The clerk or store keeps 20 to 30 percent of the transaction and the customer gets the remaining 70 percent. No goods, in reality, are ever purchased. According to sources, Terrorist organizations are attempting to counterfeit the EBT cards like they counterfeit a credit card.

Other Crimes That Make Money for Terrorists

When it comes to crimes and terrorists, there is always another way of making money. Here are a few other crimes that are becoming more popular for terrorists and terrorist funding cells to make a large amount of illegal untraceable money:

✓ **ATM Fraud**
✓ **Distribution of old candy and food products**
✓ **Counterfeit Food Products**
✓ **Counterfeit Postage Stamps**
✓ **Intellectual Property Crimes** *(Counterfeiting of clothing and products in violation of the Trademark and Copyright laws)*
✓ **Money Laundering**
✓ **Staged Accidents**
✓ **Stolen Property Fencing Operations**
✓ **Video/audio piracy**

Community Policing and
Counter-Terrorism

Community policing has a big advantage over other aspects of policing when it comes to uncovering terrorists. A Community Police Officer, when deploying correctly, becomes very familiar with local citizens and merchants. In fact, many community-policing officers become regular sounding boards for local citizens and busybodies. These citizens know a lot! Information is usually abundant. It is up to the officer to adhere to the three rules of information when receiving it (Acquisition, Analysis, Dissemination).

While much of the information may be about crime and quality of life infractions, there may be information indicating terrorist activity or terrorist profile traits. Community members want to tell someone, often a Police Officer, about disturbing rhetoric against the United States, or a certain group of people. Sometimes, it is up to the law enforcement officer to ask people in the communities. The **Knock and Talk** method can be very useful and practical in gathering this type of information. This information must be expeditiously investigated, analyzed and disseminated.

Many times, terrorist related information might be subtle or covert in nature. A law enforcement officer must be aware of crimes committed by terrorists or crimes with terrorist indicators. These indicators were discussed in a preceding chapter titled, ***Be Aware of Terrorist Indicators.*** Keep in mind the fish bowl theory of Community Policing. Communities are like fish bowls. These fish bowls have many fish, or residents, swimming around, day after day, passing each other frequently. While passing each other, day after day, all hours of the day and night, information is exchanged. These residents become monitors, in a sense, of each other. A good community police officer will be able to extract useful information from these residents and further develop the information through analysis and investigation. Remember, terrorists live and operate in communities. No matter how much they try to blend in or be anonymous, they are under the scrutiny of someone else in that community. Block watchers, busybodies, alert citizens, retired law enforcement, military personnel, or regular citizens, are monitoring each other, purposely or inadvertently. Every law enforcement officer should tap into their own communities and elicit information from as many sources as possible.

Deconfliction

Before embarking on counter-terrorism investigations, consider ongoing investigations that may be compromised in your jurisdiction. Many federal agencies and terrorist task force units are presently conducting investigations. The last thing any law enforcement officer wants to do is compromise a terrorism investigation. The best way to avoid compromising an existing investigation, or conducting conflicting cases, is to develop a local networking module with local, state and federal law enforcement agencies to discuss investigative and enforcement endeavors to combat terrorism. When law enforcement officers from all agencies work in such a close team-concept group, information is more freely shared. As a result, stepping on each other's cases can be avoided and the coordination of effort and information enhances investigations. These networking modules should have built-in deconfliction protocol. **Deconfliction**, in essence, means avoiding conflict. Deconfliction can be deployed with declassified and confidential investigations.

Another way of avoiding conflict and compromising investigations is the utilization of federal coordinating databases. One database is the Drug Enforcement Administrations DECS. DECS is Drug Enforcement Coordinating System created by the DEA. It was developed in high drug trafficking areas, such as New York City and

Miami, to coordinate drug investigations and avoid conflict in those investigations. It also maintains a sense of safety since cases are entered into the system prior to deployment of undercover officers, informants or personnel. There is nothing worse than executing a search warrant on a building where there are undercover officers involved in drug buys while arrest teams are making entry. The results can be devastating. Many undercover officers, prior to the creation of DECS, have been injured or compromised.

The Department of the Treasury embarked on a similar system for Treasury related investigations such as firearms trafficking. This system is known as TECS (Treasury

Enforcement Communications System). In addition to DECS and TECs is the Violent Gang and Terrorist Organization File (VGTOF). VGTOF is a database filled with identified members of violent gangs and terrorist organizations. It is easily accessed through NCIC (National Crime Information Center).

Funding Terrorism and the
Money Trail *or Not?*

Terrorist groups are very careful to hide the trail of money leading from, and to, their organization. They are adept at raising money from wealthy donors and Islamic charities to finance terrorist cells in more than 40 countries. Following the September 11 attacks in the United States, governments have sought ways to stop the flow of money to terrorist organizations. That effort has thrown a spotlight on "**hawala**," an informal banking system common throughout the Middle East that is used to transfer billions of dollars every year. Hawala has been utilized for many years to move terrorist money without a trace of banking records or currency transaction reports (CTR). This system makes it easy for money launderers to secretly hide and send money out of the country and avoid detection.

Operation Green Quest, a multi-agency terrorist financing task force, was established in October 2001 to identify, disrupt, and dismantle terrorist financing networks by bringing together the financial expertise from Treasury and other branches of the government. Through their investigations, Operation Green Quest agents have been targeting a wide variety of systems that may be used by terrorists to raise and move funds. These systems include illegal enterprises, as well as legitimate enterprises, and charity/relief organizations (in which donations may be diverted to terrorist groups). Green Quest's work, in cooperation with the Department of Justice, has led to 38 arrests, 26 indictments, the seizure of approximately $6.8 million domestically, and seizures of over $16 million in outbound currency at the borders, including more than $7 million in bulk cash being smuggled illegally to Middle Eastern destinations. Millions of dollars have been proven to be directly sent to al-Qaeda to fund operations leading to, and directly related to, the September 11, 2001 attacks.

To investigate local charities suspected of funding terrorism, law enforcement officers can contact agencies promoting transparency of such charities. Such agencies include the Philanthropic Research Institute, whose Guidestar organization maintains a database containing IRS filings and other financial information of over 200,000 charities. Any interested individual can access the information at **www.guidestar.org**. Another donor-information organization, the Better Business Bureau (BBB) Wise Giving Alliance, focuses on organizations that conduct broad-based fund-raising appeals. It collects and distributes information about the programs, governance, fund-raising practices, and finances of hundreds of nationally soliciting charitable organizations that are the subject of donor inquiries. It asks the selected organizations for information about their programs, governance, fund-raising practices, and finances, and measures the results against general guidelines and standards it has developed for measuring organizational efficiency and effectiveness. It publishes the results, including whether the selected organization refused to supply information, on its website at **www.give.org**.

The Holy Land Foundation for Relief and Development

On December 4, 2001, President Bush announced that the FBI and the Treasury Department had moved to seize the assets of The Holy Land Foundation for Relief and Development (HLF), beginning with their offices in Texas, California, New Jersey and Illinois. The action is a part of the administration's policy designed to choke off financial support in the war on global terrorism. Treasury Department Secretary Paul O'Neill named the HLF, as well as two Palestinian-based financial organizations, as "**Hamas** operated organizations." President Bush described Hamas as "one of the deadliest terrorist organizations in the world today," which seeks the total destruction of the State of Israel.

Various government bodies and agencies have been scrutinizing the HLF for several years. Efforts were actually stepped up just before September 11th terror attacks on New York and Washington, D.C. when the FBI raided InfoCom Corporation, an Internet service provider run by Holy Land's chairman, Ghassan Elashi, and owned by his brother Bayan Elashi, a founder and board member of the Holy Land Foundation. These efforts became part of the administration's war on terror following the September attack. The terror attacks on Israeli civilians, taken credit for by Hamas, prompted the administration to intensify its already serious approach to cracking down on the terrorists' financial infrastructure.

Source: Anti Defamation League
(http://www.adl.org/israel/holyland.asp)

Pay Attention to Details

How many times across America have law enforcement officers conducted a stop of a person on the street, in a home or business, or in a vehicle? What are the possibilities of that person being involved in terrorism? How many times are their identification documents carefully examined? How many times are they verified through computer databases or government agencies? What does a fraudulent identification document look like, anyway? What should we look for? What should we ask?

Terrorists frequently use fraudulent documents or fraudulently obtained documents such as driver's licenses, passports, state identification cards and alien cards. Timothy

Seized counterfeit Social Security card

McVeigh fraudulently obtained an Arkansas driver's license under the name Timothy Tuttle with the date of birth other than his own. He used the date, April 19, 1968. His real birth date is April 23, 1968. McVeigh used the date April 19 because it was the date he was going to bomb the Edward P. Murrah building in Oklahoma City, Oklahoma. It was also the date

51

the FBI headquarters was bombed in the white supremacist cult book, *The Turner Diaries*, written by racist William Pierce under the pseudonym, Andrew MacDonald. Although the driver's license McVeigh carried was a legitimate driver's license it was fraudulently obtained when McVeigh used a bogus date of birth.

Maybe a series of questions, tactically asked by a law enforcement officer, would result in answers revealing the

Within days of September 11, 2001, a police officer carefully examines the documents of a truck driver.

truth and in contrast to the information on the license. Maybe a consent search on the person of a suspect would result in the discovery of conflicting identification such as a credit card or a library card. When a law enforcement officer establishes a routine of questioning with careful attention to details, he or she will increase the success rate for uncovering fraud.

Paying attention to details also includes the careful examination of a document for alterations. Many times, terrorist forgers will retype information on a document to hide the real information from a law enforcement officer. Obvious forgeries include the use of whiteout, typing over a word, erasures or photocopies. Many documents, such as driver's licenses, are created with built in anti-forgery features. Holograms, code numbers and barcodes are some of these features. Even professional quality forgers find it extremely difficult to duplicate these features on a bogus document. To detect government fakes, get a detection viewer like the 3M viewer pictured.

Other examples of fakes, forgeries and counterfeiting are those of extremist groups that purchase or create their own government documents. **Washitaw Nation** and their fake driver's licenses, and license plates, is an example of an extremist group with anti-American ideology. They hide under the statement of 'freedom' but really mean to ignore the laws of the United States. In the next chapter, "*Americans Against America!*" a variety of groups is explained and their practices are exposed to avoid using US laws in everyday life.

Even counterfeit license plates are becoming more common today. In Forest Grove, Oregon, Police discovered a forgery of an Oregon license plate. The license plate was a cardboard replica of a real Oregon plate. Extremely common, is the use of fraudulent temporary license tags and imitation temporary license tags. Keep in mind, any legitimate license tag, permanent or temporary, will have corresponding paperwork from an issuing government agency or an authorized corporation. Examine the examples of fraudulent and non-US Government vehicle registration items:

ALLODIAL TITLE RECORDED A
ARAPAHOE COUNTY, COLORAI
CLERK & RECORDER'S OFFICI

7989 47

BOOK   PAGE

*Fake temporary
license tag*

British West Indies

ABC-1234

*Facsimile of a British West Indies
License Plate purchased via a
Travel Agency. Not valid in US*

Americans Against America

There is an increasing undercurrent of anti-American advocators within the borders of the United States and they are, in fact, American citizens. Many people in this category, will, most likely, refrain from the use of violence. There are those who fit this category who will engage in violence to fight against law enforcement efforts to enforce US laws. These people do not consider the laws of the United States to have any validity or authority on them. An example of such groups is the **Washitaw Nation**, **Aryan Nations**, **(David Koresch's) Branch Davidians** (Waco, Texas) and the **Randy Weaver Family** (Ruby Ridge, Idaho).

The following text has been taken from literature seized from a group advocating ignoring US laws, non-payment of taxes and anti-law enforcement opinions. These pages illustrate how to avoid identification, avoid taxes, and avoid detection from law enforcement/government officials through the use of tactics, techniques and deception. In the following, the US Government is referred to as *Terrocrats*.

Pay extra attention to the terms and tactics highlighted in **boldface**:

In determining how to deal with the car-registration issue, the first step is to decide whether you want to follow a **stand-up-and-fight** strategy, or an **invisibility strategy**.

Some brave freedom-lovers follow a stand-up-and-fight strategy by **not registering their cars**. Instead of a number plate, they may have a sign that says, for example, "**State Citizen**." They tend to not have "official" driver's licenses. They may carry with them a card with a list of case sites related to the **Right to Travel**.

To ultimately defeat the **terrocrats**, we need some brave people to openly fight them on a range of issues. If you're one of these brave people, and you're willing to do your legal homework, then you should seriously consider the stand-up-and-fight strategy. You, of course, need to be willing to be pulled over by cops, hassled, jailed, have your car confiscated, etc.

If your overall strategy includes **hunting terrocrats for fun and profit**, then you hope they'll hassle you so you can sue them and collect a payoff.

Whatever strategy you follow, you need to be aware of the implications and consequences, and you need to be ready to deal with them.

XXXX Writes:
"We have a British West Indies license plate on one of our cars. We ordered it through Rightway Travel Association. About 11:30 last night, a police officer came to our door. He asked to talk to my husband. He did mention he was not familiar with this particular plate and asked where it was from.

"This particular officer did not seem interested in the British West Indies paperwork when my husband offered to show it to him. He informed my husband the registration was overdue and he could have the car towed since it was parked on the street. He told my husband to get the temporary registration slip from the DMV and tape it in the window and the car wouldn't be towed. For you nitpickers out there, these were the particular terms the officer used.

"It did not appear to matter to him what my husband told him about the BWI registration.

"I believe the problem is with this individual officer. We have had this plate for over nine months now and have never had a problem with it until now. We live on a well-traveled street and police officers see it all the time.

"About a minute before the officer rang the door bell, a police dispatcher left a message on our machine. She identified herself as the "Name of City Police. Please pick up the phone."

"I would greatly appreciate any assistance any of you on this list could offer on what we can do when and if this officer returns."

Immediate Analysis
1. It's not clear whether you're following a stand-up-and-fight strategy or not. The fact that you're asking for assistance indicates that you haven't prepared in advance for dealing with the consequences of using the BWI registration.

2. If you want to stand up and fight, then you should immediately get competent legal assistance from someone like XXXXXXX or his contacts, or from Right Way L.A.W. –
www.livefree.com/rightwaylaw/index.html

General Considerations

1. For maximum invisibility you want a car that doesn't attract attention -- an "average" or "normal" car for your neighborhood. Have only a rear license plate. In general, park your car so the license plate isn't easily visible. (Unless you deliberately want to attract the attention of terrocrats, it's pure folly to habitually park a car with BWI plates on the street in front of your house.)

2. For maximum invisibility, **never register a car in your own name**. In many US states, possibly all, you can simply make up a "company name" like "Acme Leasing" and register the car in that name. Or you can create a trust/company with the name of your choice. So it's not your car, it's a company car, a leased car. To handle insurance you may need a lease agreement for some insurance agents. **The company address could be a mail drop.**

3. There are some cities, like Las Vegas (tourists) and Phoenix (snowbirds), where you can have an **out-of-state registration** without attracting undue attention. For company-owned cars out-of-state registration is perfectly legal in terms of terrocrat systems. In some cases you can

register a car out of state, by phone and mail, without having to go there, and without needing a local address. Call the DMV in Unita County, Wyoming – or wherever – and ask them for their out-of-state registration requirements and procedures. Some DMV terrocrats "need and want" your money. (For many years I drove a car registered in Wyoming, where insurance used to be voluntary.)

4. If you follow a stand-up-and-fight strategy, you need to be fully prepared for the consequences – your contingency plans need to be in place.

5. An important consideration is: "What can you practically get away with?" When I lived in London, England, I bought a car, **kept the plates of the previous owner**, and put a notice on the windscreen, **"License Applied For."** Once I was pulled over by a cop. He asked when I had applied for a license. I told him, three weeks ago. No further problems. In Brussels, Belgium I drove a car with old UK plates and no insurance for many years. Never pulled over; no problems. For a few years, I also drove a car with Swiss tourist plates. One afternoon an observant cop pulled me over. He must have seen me going in the

opposite direction in the morning. He asked me if I was working in Belgium. I told him I was a tourist just traveling through. After a few more questions and appropriate answers he was satisfied. Thereafter I varied my route. No further problems.

6. Some patriots claim that driver's license/car registration subjects you to terrorcrat jurisdiction and authority. Cars can be registered in trust/company names. In Phoenix, according to the driver's license application, you sign to signify that the information on the application is correct; that's it. **The address on your driver's license could be a maildrop.**

7. A general philosophical question: To what extent do you kowtow to terrocrats? **Just by putting gas in your car, you pay taxes, which finance terrocrats.** Where do you draw the line? It's a matter of individual choice. It depends on your comfort zone and expertise in dealing with terrocrats. In general, Freedom Technology enables you to greatly reduce the extent to which you kowtow to terrocrats.

8. A BWI license plate, or anything similar, could signal to a cop, "This is one of these patriot scofflaw

rebels. I'm going to show him who's boss. He'd better obey the law like everybody, or else..."

Terrorcratia:
"As yet my luck has held, and I have yet endured a battle. What I desire is to take precautionary measures to reduce or eliminate the opportunity for such a battle. I am particularly opposed to the gradual enslavement of we, the masses. My concern grows each day as I encounter more and more 'terrorcrats' who demand 'proper identification'–that usually being some sort of state or federally issued document.

"My request is simple. I seek whatever points you have to make to assist me in **becoming invisible to these parasites**. I am unaware if you have any documents available [either electronic or paper]; if so I wish to be pointed to them."

General Considerations
1. According to common law, you can use whatever name you wish, provided you don't defraud anyone.

2. In many situations **bureaucrazies** are much more interested in your "papers" than in you as an individual. If your "papers" are in order then

everything's OK. An important aspect of **Freedom Technology** is to always have the appropriate "papers" to present to bureaucrazies, so they'll leave you alone.

3. For catching a plane, staying at an hotel, renting a car, opening a bank account, etc. a wide range of types of ID cards are commonly accepted.

4. In certain situations, having the right "papers" can be a matter of life or death. Emphasis: HAVING THE RIGHT "PAPERS" CAN BE AN ISSUE OF LIFE OR DEATH!

5. To educate yourself and acquire "papers," utilize the resources below.

Resources
1. Loompanics Unlimited, PO Box 1197, Port Townsend, WA 98368 – excellent publications on **"papers"** – send $3 for catalog. Website: www.loompanics.com/

2. Porter/Terra Libra Documents, PO Box 32, Windsor, CO 80550 – **passports and vehicle operator certificates** – write for info.

3. Scope International Limited – http://www.britnet.co.uk./scope/ – publications, passports, etc.

4. World Service Authority – www.worldcitizen.org – passports, etc.

5. Rightway Travel Association, 7425 E. Lliff Ave #309, Denver, CO (80231) – 303-595-5896 – provides documents including **car registration from Washitaw Nation** – 318-343-3670. Website: http://www.rightwaylaw.com/.

6. Peugot Sound – 408-732-1776 – insurance services for Christians.

Counter-Terrorism Duty Techniques

Keep in mind, any law enforcement officer can potentially come in contact with a terrorist at any time, whether investigating an unrelated crime, conducting normal duties, or responding as a back-up for another law enforcement officer. Also, keep in mind how many of the 9-11-01 hijackers had contact with law enforcement officers in various parts of the country and how many unsuspecting law enforcement officers, in any capacity, may have such contact with terrorists today or in the future. Keep in mind the following traffic stops of the suicide pilots prior to 9-11-01:

Sept. 9, 2001
Ziad Jarrah, hijacker of the plane that crashed in Shanksville, Pennsylvania, was stopped by police in Maryland for speeding. He was driving 90 mph in a 65 mph zone. He was issued a ticket and released.

August 2001
Hani Hanjour, who hijacked & piloted the plane that crashed into the Pentagon, killing 189 persons, was stopped by police in Arlington, Virginia. He was issued a ticket for speeding and released. He paid the ticket so he would not have to show up in court.

Mohammed Atta, who hijacked and piloted the plane that crashed into the north tower of the World Trade Center, was stopped in Tamarac, Florida, for driving without a valid license and issued a ticket. He didn't pay the ticket so an arrest warrant was issued. A few weeks later he was stopped for speeding but let go because police did not know about the warrant.

Here are some techniques that will counter terrorism:

- ✓ Get to know your duty or patrol area
- ✓ Be aware of persons or activity that are out of the ordinary
- ✓ Question people and pay attention to their reaction, behavior and subsequent actions
- ✓ Create an anti-terrorism system of duty
- ✓ Identify potential targets in your area, such as:

  - **Houses of Worship**
  - **Large Public Places such as malls, stadiums and arenas**
  - **Power Plants**
  - **Government Buildings**
  - **Water Supply and Reservoirs**
  - **Water Treatment Facilities**
  - **Transportation Facilities**

- ✓ Conduct Interdiction and Investigation endeavors
- ✓ Challenge situations and persons you feel are questionable
- ✓ Attempt to identify false or fraudulent documents
- ✓ Investigate vehicles with numerous tickets
- ✓ Investigate vehicles parked for a long period of time
- ✓ Investigate unattended packages
- ✓ Investigate suspicious behavior

- ✓ Establish community contacts
- ✓ Be aware of current events, foreign and domestic
- ✓ Consider the effect on your area of assignment.
- ✓ Be alert to Religious and Public Holidays
- ✓ Read Daily Periodicals and view television news
- ✓ Continually confer with members of the community
- ✓ Stay informed on your agency's memos and procedures
- ✓ Be thorough and accurate in recording details:

- **Thoroughly describe the person(s) involved**
- **Properly identify them when possible**
- **Carefully scrutinize all documents and credentials for authenticity**
- **Pay attention to the answers given by the person you are interviewing**
- **Pay attention/verify their knowledge of their own documents**
- **Include actions of suspected persons along with specific locations and time of observation**

Investigating Terrorist Leads

Leads on terrorism can be called in from a variety of sources. Many times, the lead is called in by a nosy neighbor or concerned citizen. Every lead must be investigated thoroughly. That nosy neighbor may have that one bit of information that starts a major criminal or terrorism investigation or leads to a plot to kill someone or blow up a building. Every law enforcement officer should pay extra attention to a tip or lead mentioning:

❑ *Suspicious persons involved in clandestine martial arts or defensive tactics training*

❑ *Suspicious or unauthorized persons attempting to acquire weapons*

❑ *Late night meetings involving suspicious persons*

❑ *Apparent wealth with no apparent means of income*

❑ *A company claiming enormous income with minimal business*

❑ *Strange purchases of potential explosive devices, mixtures or parts*

❑ *Suspicious or unauthorized persons attempting to buy law enforcement or security uniforms*

❑ *Suspicious persons attempting to buy out-of-service police or emergency vehicles*

❑ *Recent theft of identification items such as immigration documents, drivers' licenses, passports and state ID cards*

❑ *A suspicious person purchasing a vehicle with fake identification*

Suspicious Packages and Dangerous Compounds

Here are graphics, compliments of the Bureau Alcohol Tobacco and Firearms, to help identify suspicious packages that may be, in fact, terrorist bombs or bomb components:

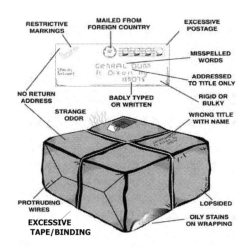

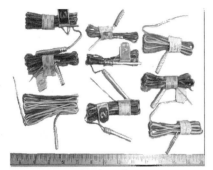

Blasting Caps

*Plastic
Explosives*

Detonation Cord

Soviet Suitcase
Nuclear Bomb

Ammonium Nitrate and
Fuel Oil (ANFO)

Safety and Survival

While fighting terrorism, every law enforcement officer must remain alert at all times. Terrorists are extremely adept at counter-surveillance and have a big advantage over us. They operate clandestinely and tend to blend in to their surroundings. Law enforcement officers, for the most part, do not! While many law enforcement officers wear uniforms, display identification, work at known law enforcement facilities, or utilize vehicles that are dead give-aways, terrorists take extra care to hide their true identity or job.

Every law enforcement officer should be aware of counter-surveillance and terrorist back-up cells and conscientiously practice safety and awareness techniques. These techniques should include:

- ✓ Prepare for daily duties and assignments
- ✓ Always wear a ballistic vest
- ✓ Carry the proper equipment
- ✓ Ensure your equipment is in proper working order
- ✓ Fully pre-investigate leads you are assigned by:

  - • *Checking the location and person involved via available databases and information archives*
  - • *Verify if the location or person is the subject of other leads or investigations*

- ✓ Conduct careful surveillance of lead locations and suspected terrorist locations prior to visiting
- ✓ Practice alertness and cognizance of surroundings
- ✓ Use caution and good judgment before entering
- ✓ Pay attention to terrorist indicators
- ✓ Be alert to suspicious packages and dangerous compounds
- ✓ Familiarize yourself with *Instructions for the Suicide Martyr for the Last Night* located in this book
- ✓ Be alert to surveillance on you!
- ✓ If you do not feel safe, you can always retreat and come back again with plenty of reinforcements

Suggested Tools for the War on Terror

1. Binoculars
2. Camera (Instant or Digital)
3. Cassette recorder (mini)
4. Chem/Bio decontamination kit
5. Coveralls
6. ID/Driver's License Checking Guide
7. ID Viewer (lighted)
8. Magnifying Glass
9. Emergency Breathing Mask
10. Flashlight
11. Fluorescent Light
12. Forceps
13. Magnifying (Lighted) Glass
14. Rubber Gloves
15. Radiation Scanner (portable)

Terrorist/Potential Incidents
Since 9-11-01

Legend: (*gathered from a variety of sources*)
   (Incidents indicated on map with a Diamond ◆)

1. **Tacoma, Washington:** Stolen Identification Stamps used to approve Visas and Extensions in the country.
2. **San Pedro, California:** Potential Terrorist Sympathizers smuggling weapons on a Merchant Marine Vessel.
3. **Buffalo, New York:** 6 members of al-Qaeda terrorist cell are arrested.
4. **Seattle, Washington**: 4 members of al-Qaeda arrested.
5. **Bronx (NYC), New York**: 2 possible terrorist cell members arrested with bomb-making devices (jars and det cord).
6. **New York City, New York**: Gunman fires gun at the United Nations.
7. **Los Angeles, California**: Gunman fires gun in LAX airport killing two people.
8. **Miami, Florida:** Richard Reid attempts to blow up plane enroute to Miami but is subdued by crew and passengers.

9. **Ft. Worth, Texas**: (September 12, 2001) Two men were arrested on an Amtrak Train for carrying $5,000 in cash, boxcutters and hair dye.

10. **Utah:** Two suspected al-Qaeda members were arrested on I-70 in possession of $300K in cash.

11. **Omaha, Nebraska**: Two men were stopped by police and turned over to federal authorities. They were later charged with funneling money to terrorists.

12. **Bly, Oregon**: An al-Qaeda terrorist training camp was identified.

13. **Reno, Nevada**: Lucas Helder, the 'happy face' pipe-bomber, was arrested.

14. **Colorado Springs, Colorado:** Chemical & Biological weapons devices were stolen from the University of Colorado.

15. **Joliet, Illinois**: 1,000 pounds of Zirconium pellets stolen.

16. **St. Louis, Missouri:** Surveillance photos were taken of bridges and buildings.

17. **Detroit, Michigan**: Smuggled Muslims out of the US into Canada.

18. **New York City, New York:** Threat of a Nerve Gas attack in the subway system.

19. **Washington, DC:** Threat of a Nerve Gas attack in the subway system.

20. **New York, New Jersey Region**: Suspected terrorist related inquiries made into renting and purchasing ambulances.
21. **Miami, Florida:** 5,500 Stolen Florida Drivers' Licenses.
22. **Los Angeles, California**: Surveillance photos taken of large Cruise Ships.
23. **Waverly, Nebraska**: Suspected terrorist attempt to purchase a fuel truck.
24. **Buffalo, New York:** Suspected terrorists threaten to dump Cyanide into St. Lawrence River.
25. **Dallas, Texas:** Suspected terrorist sympathizers attempt to purchase police uniforms.
26. **Ocean County, New Jersey**: 160 two-way radios stolen.
27. **Denver, Colorado**: Muslim radical male arrested with plans to poison water supplies.
28. **Dearborn, Michigan**: Man arrested with $12 million in counterfeit checks.
29. **Charlotte, North Carolina**: Suspected terrorist funding supporters arrested for smuggling millions of dollars of untaxed cigarettes.
30. **Memphis, Tennessee**: Five potential terrorist supporters arrested in driver's license fraud ring.

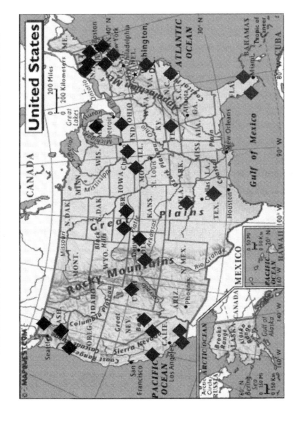

The Indicators Leading to September 11, 2001

✓ **1989:** Ali Mohammed, an Egyptian Military lateral into the US Special Forces, was a Sergeant in the US Army, assigned to Ft Bragg, who was later uncovered as a member of the Egyptian Jihad terrorist organization and top aide to Osama bin Laden. He stole documents, some of which were classified Secret, that contained the locations of U.S. military Special Operations Forces exercises and units in the Middle East, military training. According to transcripts of the World Trade Center bombing trials, Ali Mohammed began giving training sessions in New Jersey in guerilla warfare in 1989 to Islamic militants that included among others, El Sayyid Nosair, Mahmud Abuhalima (later convicted in the World Trade Center bombing conspiracy) and Khalid Ibrahim.

✓ **1988 to 1990:** Several Islamic radicals trained by a retired police officer at a Waterbury, CT firearms range, one of whom was El Sayyid Nosair, would use firearms supplied by the range officer and AK47s they brought themselves.

- ✓ **November 1990:** Rabbi Meir Kahane was gunned down by El Sayyid Nosair, a member of Egyptian Jihad.
- ✓ **November 1990:** El Sayyid Nosair's apartment in NJ contained numerous documents indicating a terrorist plot against the US. There was a quote in the documents stating: ***"destroy the large buildings that the Americans love so much…"*** These documents were not thoroughly examined until after the World Trade Center bombing in 1993.
- ✓ **November 1990:** Documents seized from El Sayyid Nosair's apartment in the Middle East revealed secret US Military documents stolen from Ft. Bragg.
- ✓ **January 1993:** One of Germany's highest-ranking intelligence officials, on an undisclosed visit to Washington, warned his Federal counterparts that radical Islamic fundamentalists had relocated to the West and constituted a major new terrorist threat to the United States and Europe.
- ✓ **February 26, 1993:** World Trade Center bombing by Ramzi Yusef and members of his terrorist cell. Six people killed and 1,000 wounded.
- ✓ **1994:** In the first WTC bombing one of the conspirators Nidal Ayyad was identified as a Rutgers University-trained chemist working for Allied Signal in New Jersey at the time of his arrest.

Ayyad was convicted **in 1994** but left the following warning on his hard drive...*"Next time it will be very precise."*

✓ **1995:** Project "BOJINKA"- Bin Laden plot by Ramzi Youssef was uncovered in Philippines when an apartment where bombs are being assembled caught on fire. The plot was to bomb 12 US airliners in one day while enroute to the USA.

✓ **1996:** It was confirmed that al-Qaeda operative, Abdul Hakim Murad, had trained at the same flight school in Oklahoma, as Moussaoui, as part of preparations for a suicide hijack attack on CIA headquarters. Murad testified about these plans in the 1996 trial of Ramzi Yusef, who was the organizer of the 1993 World Trade Center bombing.

✓ **1996:** Marseilles, France. A hijacking took place of Air France Flight 8969. The hijackers were planning to fly the plane into the Eiffel Tower. They couldn't complete their plan because the hijackers were not trained to fly the airliner.

✓ **July 31, 1997:** Ghazi Ibrahim Abu Mezer and Lafi Khalil were arrested in Brooklyn, NY by police officers from the NYPD. The arrest was based on a tip that people in the apartment were intending to bomb the New York subway system.

✓ **August 1997:** During a raid on **Wadih El Hage**'s house, the FBI recovered a **letter** from his personal computer. It was written by Haroun Fazul, one of the suspects in the Nairobi bombing who had stayed in **El Hage**'s house. In the **letter**, Haroun expresses concern that the cell members in East Africa are in great danger from American intelligence forces, and asks, *"Are we ready for that big clandestine battle?"*

✓ **February 1998:** Saudi dissident Mohammed al-Massari and Omar **Bakri**, leader of al-Muhajiroun, signed a statement calling for attacks on American targets. Sixty UK groups added their names. Two weeks later, Bin Laden echoed the call. "In compliance with God's order," read the fax released from his London office, "we issue the following fatwa to all Muslims to kill the Americans." Months later, two US embassies in East Africa were bombed.

✓ **February 23, 1998:** Bin Laden issued a fatwa (an Islamic religious ruling) calling for Muslims to kill Americans and Jews anywhere in the world. The fatwa concluded with, *"[W]e - with God's help - call on every Muslim who believes in God and wishes to be rewarded to comply with God's order to kill Americans and plunder their money wherever and whenever they find it."* The fatwa was issued under the name of a new organization, the "International Islamic Front Against the Jews and the Crusaders." Signing along with Bin Laden were other members of the new Front's leadership: Ayman al-Zawahiri, leader of Egyptian Jihad; Abu-Yasir Rifa'i Ahmad Taha, leader of the Egyptian Al-Gama'a Al-Islamiya; Sheikh Mir Hamzah, secretary of the Jamia-ul-Ulema-e-Pakistan; and Fazul Rahman of the Jihad movement in Bangladesh.

✓ **August 28, 1998:** From jail, Sheikh Mohammad Omar Abdel Rahman pronounced a "fatwa" for waging a holy war against the US. Sheikh Rahman, an Egyptian cleric, is currently serving a prison term in New York for his alleged role in the 1993 bombing of the World Trade Center. He is quoted as saying, *"Spoil their trade, burn their companies, drown their boats and target their planes and kill them on the land, in the oceans and in the air: from your brother in American prison Omar Abdul Rahman,"* the message said. *"Allah will help you against them,"* the message read.

✓ **September 1998:** Ali Muhammad, whose real name is Abu al Sa'ud, was in custody on federal charges stemming from his theft of secret Military documents from Ft. Bragg where he was assigned as a supply Sergeant with the US Army. Ali Muhammad was a top aide to Osama bin Laden.

✓ Since late **1998:** The following radical groups were active in the United States:

- ○ **Hamas**
- ○ **Islamic Jihad**
- ○ **Hizballah**
- ○ **Hizba-Tahrir (Islamic Liberation Party)**
- ○ **Armed Islamic Group (GIA)**
- ○ **En-Nahda**
- ○ **Muslim Brotherhood**
- ○ **Al-Gama'a Islamiyya**
- ○ **Al-Qaeda**

✓ **July 20, 1999:** Ahmad Salame Mabruk, an aide to Osama bin Laden, and military leader of Egyptian Islamic Jihad, was arrested in Azerbaijan for trying to buy chemical and biological weapons. In his possession was a computer disk listing over one hundred targets in the US, Israel and India.

✓ **August, 1999:** A specific threat to attack Washington DC by Bin Laden's group was uncovered. 40 members of al-Qaeda were identified by name operating in two different cells out of New York City and Washington, DC. Specific locations were identified as well as travel countries of origin were identified. The attack was intercepted and interdicted by US and foreign authorities.

✓ **December 14, 1999:** US Customs Officials arrested an Algerian national and suspected GIA militant, Ahmed Ressam, for transporting bomb-making materials from Canada into the US. Charged with possession of bomb-making materials, use of false identification, resisting arrest, and making false statements to US officials. He was trained in camps run by Islamic militants fighting the Russians in Afghanistan during the 1980s.

✓ **September 2000:** Captain Rasul Parwaz, a former pilot with Afghanistan's national airline, Ariana, stated that he had helped train 14 Islamic militants, some holding European passports, to fly civilian aircraft at a Taliban training facility in the city of Bamiyan, in Afghanistan. The pilot said that the trainees, whom he described as "fanatics," had left Afghanistan nearly one year ago to undisclosed locations after they completed their training. The trainees were Pakistanis, Afghans and Arab nationals. Some carried European passports and spoke fluent English. Other instructors included a retired Pakistani general. Captain Parwaz stated that seven of the trainees spoke English well enough to translate flying manuals into Farsi, Urdu and Pushtun.

✓ **Late 2000:** Taha Musa of the Al-Gama'a al-Islamiyya appeared in a video with Osama bin-Laden threatening retaliation against the US for the incarceration of Sheik Omar Abdel Rahman.

- ✓ **Early 2001:** Federal agents conducting surveillance of two members of the Islamic Jihad terrorist organization who were crossing the border into the US from Canada were lost by the federal agents.

- ✓ **June 2001:** Federal agents in New York City arrest a man for taking pictures of government buildings. He was later released.

- ✓ **June 2001:** In New York City, federal agents arrest and release a man taking pictures of security ops at 4 downtown buildings

- ✓ **June 2001:** ID badges and uniforms are stolen from the hotel rooms of American Airline employees at the Hotel Nazionale in Rome, Italy

- ✓ **June 22, 2001:** US State Department issues a warning that Americans and American interests abroad may be the target of terrorist attacks.

- ✓ **August 2001:** Five weeks prior to the hijackings, a briefcase bearing the name of one of the suspected hijackers Hani Hanjour was found at the San Diego Zoo. The briefcase, filled with an undisclosed sum of cash and documents written in Arabic, was retrieved after it was placed in the zoo's lost and found, according to a zoo official and a federal law enforcement source. Authorities were notified of the episode *after the 9-11 attacks*. The federal source, speaking on the condition of anonymity, said the briefcase was identified as belonging to Hani Hanjour, one of three suspected hijackers who had once lived in the San Diego area and was identified by authorities as being on American Airlines Flight 77, which crashed into the Pentagon. The San Diego Zoo later came up on a credible target list.

✓ **August 17, 2001:** FBI arrested an al-Qaeda member, Zacarias Moussaoui, in St. Paul, Minnesota and received French intelligence reports linking him to Osama bin Laden. French authorities reported the man had dual French and Algerian nationality and had several passports, technical information on Boeing aircraft and flight manuals. He requested flight instruction on a 747 simulator owned by Northwest Airlines. He entered the US from London in February on a fake Moroccan passport and was heading toward flight training school in Norman, OK. He paid cash. He attempted to arrange simulator training through the Pan Am International Flight Academy in Florida.

✓ **August 24, 2001:** Intelligence sources in Pakistan reveal that fugitive Osama bin Laden has gone underground in Afghanistan amid expectations of a U.S. commando strike.

- ✓ **August and early September 2001:** Close associates of bin Laden were warned to return to Afghanistan from other parts of the world by September 10, 2001.
- ✓ **August 2001:** An Arab journalist with access to bin Laden said he had warned that his followers would carry out "an unprecedented attack… a very big one" on U.S. interests.
- ✓ **August 27, 2001:** Sources state: A coded telephone call to a Muslim cleric living in Madrid provided the first proof of Osama bin Laden's hand in the September 11 attacks. Sixteen days before the hijackings in America, an al-Qaeda agent telephoned the cleric in Madrid known as Abu Dahdah, boasting about the plot. The agent, who calls himself "Shakur," talks about how *"in our lessons, we entered the field of aviation and we cut the bird's throat."* Spanish police will say only that the call came from abroad but will not say whether it came from one of the hijackers. Three weeks earlier "Shakur" had called to say: *"I am preparing certain things which should please you."*
- ✓ **September 7, 2001:** US State Department issues a warning that Americans and American interests abroad may be the target of terrorist attacks.
- ✓ **September 8, 2001:** Arabic satellite television channel MBC warned that followers of suspected Saudi

terrorist Osama bin Laden were planning a major attack on U.S. and Israeli interests in the next two weeks.

✓ **September 10, 2001:**   Israeli Defense Minister Benjamin Ben-Eliezer also warned the day before attacks, that *"...a coalition has been formed recently between terror organizations, Palestinians, Shiites and bin Laden operating against Israeli, American and European targets."*

September 11, 2001:

World Trade Center
attacked

Pentagon

Flight 93 Crash Site, Shanksville, PA

Instructions for the Suicide Martyr
for the Last Night

Investigators found this letter handwritten in Arabic in the suitcase of Mohammad Atta. It includes Islamic prayers, instructions for the last night of life, and a practical checklist for the final suicide operation. It was released, untranslated, until the British newspaper The Observer, published this translation.

Additional copies of this letter were found at the crash site of United Airlines Flight 93 in Pennsylvania and at a Dulles International Airport parking lot in a car registered to one of the hijackers on American Flight 77.

Instructions for the Last Night:

1. MAKE AN OATH TO DIE AND RENEW YOUR INTENTIONS.
   - SHAVE EXCESS HAIR FROM THE BODY AND WEAR COLOGNE.
   - SHOWER

2. MAKE SURE YOU KNOW ALL ASPECTS OF THE PLAN WELL, AND EXPECT THE RESPONSE, OR A REACTION, FROM THE ENEMY.

3. READ AL-TAWBA AND ANFAL [TRADITIONAL WAR CHAPTERS FROM THE QUR'AN] AND REFLECT ON THEIR MEANINGS AND REMEMBER ALL OF THE THINGS GOD HAS PROMISED FOR THE MARTYRS.

4. REMIND YOUR SOUL TO LISTEN AND OBEY [ALL DIVINE ORDERS] AND REMEMBER THAT YOU WILL FACE DECISIVE SITUATIONS THAT MIGHT PREVENT YOU FROM 100 PER CENT OBEDIENCE, SO TAME YOUR SOUL, PURIFY IT, CONVINCE IT, MAKE IT UNDERSTAND, AND INCITE IT. GOD SAID: 'OBEY GOD AND HIS MESSENGER, AND DO NOT FIGHT AMONGST YOURSELVES OR ELSE YOU WILL FAIL. AND BE PATIENT, FOR GOD IS WITH THE PATIENT.'

5. PRAY DURING THE NIGHT AND BE PERSISTENT IN ASKING GOD TO GIVE YOU VICTORY, CONTROL AND CONQUEST, AND THAT HE MAY MAKE YOUR TASK EASIER AND NOT EXPOSE US.

6. REMEMBER GOD FREQUENTLY, AND THE BEST WAY TO DO IT IS TO READ THE HOLY QUR'AN, ACCORDING TO ALL SCHOLARS, AS FAR AS I KNOW. IT IS ENOUGH FOR US THAT IT [THE QUR'AN] ARE THE WORDS OF THE CREATOR OF THE EARTH AND THE PLANTS, THE ONE THAT YOU WILL MEET [ON THE DAY OF JUDGMENT].

7. PURIFY YOUR SOUL FROM ALL UNCLEAN THINGS. COMPLETELY FORGET SOMETHING CALLED 'THIS WORLD' [OR 'THIS LIFE']. THE TIME FOR PLAY IS OVER AND THE SERIOUS TIME IS UPON US. HOW MUCH TIME HAVE WE WASTED IN OUR LIVES? SHOULDN'T WE TAKE ADVANTAGE OF THESE LAST HOURS TO OFFER GOOD DEEDS AND OBEDIENCE?

8. YOU SHOULD FEEL COMPLETE TRANQUILITY, BECAUSE THE TIME BETWEEN YOU AND YOUR MARRIAGE [IN HEAVEN] IS VERY SHORT. AFTERWARDS BEGINS THE HAPPY LIFE, WHERE GOD IS SATISFIED WITH YOU, AND ETERNAL BLISS 'IN THE COMPANY OF THE PROPHETS, THE COMPANIONS, THE MARTYRS AND THE GOOD PEOPLE, WHO ARE ALL GOOD COMPANY'. ASK GOD FOR HIS MERCY AND BE OPTIMISTIC,

BECAUSE [THE PROPHET], PEACE BE UPON HIM,
USED TO PREFER OPTIMISM IN ALL HIS AFFAIRS.

9. KEEP IN MIND THAT, IF YOU FALL INTO HARDSHIP,
HOW WILL YOU ACT AND HOW WILL YOU REMAIN
STEADFAST AND REMEMBER THAT YOU WILL
RETURN TO GOD AND REMEMBER THAT ANY-
THING THAT HAPPENS TO YOU COULD NEVER BE
AVOIDED, AND WHAT DID NOT HAPPEN TO YOU
COULD NEVER HAVE HAPPENED TO YOU. THIS
TEST FROM ALMIGHTY GOD IS TO RAISE YOUR
LEVEL [LEVELS OF HEAVEN] AND ERASE YOUR
SINS. AND BE SURE THAT IT IS A MATTER OF
MOMENTS, WHICH WILL THEN PASS, GOD WILLING,
SO BLESSED ARE THOSE WHO WIN THE GREAT
REWARD OF GOD. ALMIGHTY GOD SAID: 'DID YOU
THINK YOU COULD GO TO HEAVEN BEFORE GOD
KNOWS WHOM AMONGST YOU HAVE FOUGHT FOR
HIM AND ARE PATIENT?'

10. REMEMBER THE WORDS OF ALMIGHTY GOD: 'YOU
WERE LOOKING TO THE BATTLE BEFORE YOU
ENGAGED IN IT, AND NOW YOU SEE IT WITH YOUR
OWN TWO EYES.' REMEMBER: 'HOW MANY SMALL
GROUPS BEAT BIG GROUPS BY THE WILL OF GOD.'
AND HIS WORDS: 'IF GOD GIVES YOU VICTORY, NO
ONE CAN BEAT YOU. AND IF HE BETRAYS YOU,

WHO CAN GIVE YOU VICTORY WITHOUT HIM? SO
THE FAITHFUL PUT THEIR TRUST IN GOD.'

11. REMIND YOURSELF OF THE SUPPLICATIONS AND OF
YOUR BRETHREN AND PONDER THEIR MEANINGS.
(THE MORNING AND EVENING SUPPLICATIONS,
AND THE SUPPLICATIONS OF [ENTERING] A TOWN,
AND THE [UNCLEAR] SUPPLICATIONS, AND THE
SUPPLICATIONS SAID BEFORE MEETING THE
ENEMY.)

12. BLESS YOUR BODY WITH SOME VERSES OF THE
QUR'AN [DONE BY READING VERSES INTO ONE'S
HANDS AND THEN RUBBING THE HANDS OVER
WHATEVER IS TO BE BLESSED], THE LUGGAGE,
CLOTHES, THE KNIFE, YOUR PERSONAL EFFECTS,
YOUR ID, PASSPORT, AND ALL YOUR PAPERS.

13. CHECK YOUR WEAPON BEFORE YOU LEAVE AND LONG
BEFORE YOU LEAVE. (YOU MUST MAKE YOUR
KNIFE SHARP AND MUST NOT DISCOMFORT YOUR
ANIMAL DURING THE SLAUGHTER).

14. TIGHTEN YOUR CLOTHES [A REFERENCE TO MAKING
SURE HIS CLOTHES WILL COVER HIS PRIVATE
PARTS AT ALL TIMES], SINCE THIS IS THE WAY
OF THE PIOUS GENERATIONS AFTER THE
PROPHET. THEY WOULD TIGHTEN THEIR CLOTHES
BEFORE BATTLE. TIGHTEN YOUR SHOES WELL,
WEAR SOCKS SO THAT YOUR FEET WILL BE

SOLIDLY IN YOUR SHOES. ALL OF THESE ARE WORLDLY THINGS [THAT HUMANS CAN DO TO CONTROL THEIR FATE, ALTHOUGH GOD DECREES WHAT WILL WORK AND WHAT WON'T] AND THE REST IS LEFT TO GOD, THE BEST ONE TO DEPEND ON.

15. PRAY THE MORNING PRAYER IN A GROUP AND PONDER THE GREAT REWARDS OF THAT PRAYER. MAKE SUPPLICATIONS AFTERWARDS, AND DO NOT LEAVE YOUR APARTMENT UNLESS YOU HAVE PERFORMED ABLUTION BEFORE LEAVING, BECAUSE THE ANGELS WILL ASK FOR YOUR FORGIVENESS AS LONG AS YOU ARE IN A STATE OF ABLUTION, AND WILL PRAY FOR YOU. THIS SAYING OF THE PROPHET WAS MENTIONED BY AN-NAWAWI IN HIS BOOK, THE BEST OF SUPPLICATIONS. READ THE WORDS OF GOD: 'DID YOU THINK THAT WE CREATED YOU FOR NO REASON ...' FROM THE AL-MU'MINUN CHAPTER.

Instructions for the Day of the Attack:

WHEN THE TAXI TAKES YOU TO (M) [THIS INITIAL COULD STAND FOR MATAR, AIRPORT IN ARABIC] REMEMBER GOD CONSTANTLY WHILE IN THE CAR. (REMEMBER THE SUPPLICATION FOR

ENTERING A CAR, FOR ENTERING A TOWN, THE
SUPPLICATION OF PLACE AND OTHER SUPPLI-
CATIONS).

WHEN YOU HAVE REACHED (M) AND HAVE LEFT
THE TAXI, SAY A SUPPLICATION OF PLACE ['OH
LORD, I ASK YOU FOR THE BEST OF THIS PLACE,
AND ASK YOU TO PROTECT ME FROM ITS EVILS'],
AND EVERYWHERE YOU GO SAY THAT PRAYER
AND SMILE AND BE CALM, FOR GOD IS WITH THE
BELIEVERS. AND THE ANGELS PROTECT YOU
WITHOUT YOU FEELING ANYTHING. SAY THIS
SUPPLICATION: 'GOD IS MORE DEAR THAN ALL OF
HIS CREATION.' AND SAY: 'OH LORD, PROTECT ME
FROM THEM AS YOU WISH.' AND SAY: 'OH LORD,
TAKE YOUR ANGER OUT ON [THE ENEMY] AND
WE ASK YOU TO PROTECT US FROM THEIR EVILS.'
AND SAY: 'OH LORD, BLOCK THEIR VISION FROM
IN FRONT OF THEM, SO THAT THEY MAY NOT
SEE.' AND SAY: 'GOD IS ALL WE NEED, HE IS THE
BEST TO RELY UPON.' REMEMBER GOD'S WORDS:
'THOSE TO WHOM THE PEOPLE SAID, "THE
PEOPLE HAVE GATHERED TO GET YOU, SO FEAR
THEM," BUT THAT ONLY INCREASED THEIR FAITH

AND THEY SAID, GOD IS ALL WE NEED, HE IS THE BEST TO RELY UPON.' AFTER YOU SAY THAT, YOU WILL FIND [UNCLEAR] AS GOD PROMISED THIS TO HIS SERVANTS WHO SAY THIS SUPPLICATION:

1. THEY WILL COME BACK [FROM BATTLE] WITH GOD'S BLESSINGS
2. THEY WERE NOT HARMED
3. AND GOD WAS SATISFIED WITH THEM.

GOD SAYS: 'THEY CAME BACK WITH GOD'S BLESSINGS, WERE NOT HARMED, AND GOD WAS SATISFIED WITH THEM, AND GOD IS EVER-BLESSING.'

Instructions for the Plane and the Attack:

WHEN YOU RIDE THE (T) [PROBABLY FOR TAYYARA, AEROPLANE IN ARABIC], BEFORE YOUR FOOT STEPS IN IT, AND BEFORE YOU ENTER IT, YOU MAKE A PRAYER AND SUPPLICATIONS. REMEMBER THAT THIS IS A BATTLE FOR THE SAKE OF GOD. AS THE PROPHET, PEACE BE UPON HIM, SAID, 'AN ACTION FOR THE SAKE OF GOD IS BETTER THAN ALL OF WHAT IS IN THIS WORLD.' WHEN YOU STEP INSIDE THE

(T), AND SIT IN YOUR SEAT, BEGIN WITH THE KNOWN SUPPLICATIONS THAT WE HAVE MENTIONED BEFORE. BE BUSY WITH THE CONSTANT REMEMBRANCE OF GOD. GOD SAID: 'OH YE FAITHFUL, WHEN YOU FIND THE ENEMY BE STEADFAST, AND REMEMBER GOD CONSTANTLY SO THAT YOU MAY BE SUCCESSFUL.' WHEN THE (T) MOVES, EVEN SLIGHTLY, TOWARD (Q) [UNKNOWN REFERENCE], SAY THE SUPPLICATION OF TRAVEL. BECAUSE YOU ARE TRAVELING TO ALMIGHTY GOD, SO BE ATTENTIVE ON THIS TRIP.

THEN [UNCLEAR] IT TAKES OFF. THIS IS THE MOMENT THAT BOTH GROUPS COME TOGETHER. SO REMEMBER GOD, AS HE SAID IN HIS BOOK: 'OH LORD, POUR YOUR PATIENCE UPON US AND MAKE OUR FEET STEADFAST AND GIVE US VICTORY OVER THE INFIDELS.' AND HIS WORDS: 'AND THE ONLY THING THEY SAID LORD, FORGIVE OUR SINS AND EXCESSES AND MAKE OUR FEET STEADFAST AND GIVE US VICTORY OVER THE INFIDELS.' AND HIS PROPHET SAID: 'OH LORD, YOU HAVE REVEALED THE BOOK, YOU MOVE THE CLOUDS, YOU GAVE US VICTORY OVER THE ENEMY, CONQUER THEM AND GIVE US VICTORY OVER THEM.' GIVE US VICTORY AND MAKE THE

GROUND SHAKE UNDER THEIR FEET. PRAY FOR YOURSELF AND ALL YOUR BROTHERS THAT THEY MAY BE VICTORIOUS AND HIT THEIR TARGETS AND ASK GOD TO GRANT YOU MARTYRDOM FACING THE ENEMY, NOT RUNNING AWAY FROM IT, AND FOR HIM TO GRANT YOU PATIENCE AND THE FEELING THAT ANYTHING THAT HAPPENS TO YOU IS FOR HIM.

THEN EVERY ONE OF YOU SHOULD PREPARE TO CARRY OUT HIS ROLE IN A WAY THAT WOULD SATISFY GOD. YOU SHOULD CLENCH YOUR TEETH, AS THE PIOUS EARLY GENERATIONS DID.

WHEN THE CONFRONTATION BEGINS, STRIKE LIKE CHAMPIONS WHO DO NOT WANT TO GO BACK TO THIS WORLD. SHOUT, 'ALLAHU AKBAR,' BECAUSE THIS STRIKES FEAR IN THE HEARTS OF THE NON-BELIEVERS. GOD SAID: 'STRIKE ABOVE THE NECK, AND STRIKE AT ALL OF THEIR EXTREMITIES.' KNOW THAT THE GARDENS OF PARADISE ARE WAITING FOR YOU IN ALL THEIR BEAUTY, AND THE WOMEN OF PARADISE ARE WAITING, CALLING OUT, 'COME HITHER, FRIEND OF GOD.' THEY HAVE DRESSED IN THEIR MOST BEAUTIFUL CLOTHING.

IF GOD DECREES THAT ANY OF YOU ARE TO SLAUGHTER, DEDICATE THE SLAUGHTER TO YOUR FATHERS AND [UNCLEAR], BECAUSE YOU HAVE OBLIGATIONS TOWARD THEM. DO NOT DISAGREE, AND OBEY. IF YOU SLAUGHTER, DO NOT CAUSE THE DISCOMFORT OF THOSE YOU ARE KILLING, BECAUSE THIS IS ONE OF THE PRACTICES OF THE PROPHET, PEACE BE UPON HIM. ON ONE CONDITION: THAT YOU DO NOT BECOME DISTRACTED BY [UNCLEAR] AND NEGLECT WHAT IS GREATER, PAYING ATTENTION TO THE ENEMY. THAT WOULD BE TREASON, AND WOULD DO MORE DAMAGE THAN GOOD. IF THIS HAPPENS, THE DEED AT HAND IS MORE IMPORTANT THAN DOING THAT, BECAUSE THE DEED IS AN OBLIGATION, AND [THE OTHER THING] IS OPTIONAL. AND AN OBLIGATION HAS PRIORITY OVER AN OPTION.

DO NOT SEEK REVENGE FOR YOURSELF. STRIKE FOR GOD'S SAKE. ONE TIME ALI BIN ABI TALIB [A COMPANION AND CLOSE RELATIVE OF THE PROPHET MUHAMMAD], FOUGHT WITH A NON-BELIEVER. THE NON-BELIEVER SPIT ON ALI, MAY GOD BLESS HIM. ALI [UNCLEAR] HIS SWORD, BUT DID NOT STRIKE HIM. WHEN THE BATTLE WAS OVER, THE COMPANIONS OF

THE PROPHET ASKED HIM WHY HE HAD NOT SMITTEN THE NON-BELIEVER. HE SAID, 'AFTER HE SPAT AT ME, I WAS AFRAID I WOULD BE STRIKING AT HIM IN REVENGE FOR MYSELF, SO I LIFTED MY SWORD.' AFTER HE RENEWED HIS INTENTIONS, HE WENT BACK AND KILLED THE MAN. THIS MEANS THAT BEFORE YOU DO ANYTHING, MAKE SURE YOUR SOUL IS PREPARED TO DO EVERYTHING FOR GOD ONLY.

THEN IMPLEMENT THE WAY OF THE PROPHET IN TAKING PRISONERS. TAKE PRISONERS AND KILL THEM. AS ALMIGHTY GOD SAID: 'NO PROPHET SHOULD HAVE PRISONERS UNTIL HE HAS SOAKED THE LAND WITH BLOOD. YOU WANT THE BOUNTIES OF THIS WORLD [IN EXCHANGE FOR PRISONERS] AND GOD WANTS THE OTHER WORLD [FOR YOU], AND GOD IS ALL-POWERFUL, ALL-WISE.'

IF EVERYTHING GOES WELL, EVERY ONE OF YOU SHOULD PAT THE OTHER ON THE SHOULDER IN CONFIDENCE THAT (M) AND (T) NUMBER (K). REMIND YOUR BROTHERS THAT THIS ACT IS FOR ALMIGHTY GOD. DO NOT CONFUSE YOUR BROTHERS OR DISTRACT THEM. HE SHOULD GIVE THEM GLAD

TIDINGS AND MAKE THEM CALM, AND REMIND THEM
[OF GOD] AND ENCOURAGE THEM. HOW BEAUTIFUL
IT IS FOR ONE TO READ GOD'S WORDS, SUCH AS: 'AND
THOSE WHO PREFER THE AFTERLIFE OVER THIS
WORLD SHOULD FIGHT FOR THE SAKE OF GOD.' AND
HIS WORDS: 'DO NOT SUPPOSE THAT THOSE WHO ARE
KILLED FOR THE SAKE OF GOD ARE DEAD; THEY ARE
ALIVE ... ' AND OTHERS. OR THEY SHOULD SING
SONGS TO BOOST THEIR MORALE, AS THE PIOUS
FIRST GENERATIONS DID IN THE THROES OF BATTLE,
TO BRING CALM, TRANQUILLITY AND JOY TO THE
HEARTS OF HIS BROTHERS.

DO NOT FORGET TO TAKE A BOUNTY, EVEN IF IT IS A
GLASS OF WATER TO QUENCH YOUR THIRST OR THAT
OF YOUR BROTHERS, IF POSSIBLE. WHEN THE HOUR
OF REALITY APPROACHES, THE ZERO HOUR,
[UNCLEAR] AND WHOLEHEARTEDLY WELCOME
DEATH FOR THE SAKE OF GOD. ALWAYS BE
REMEMBERING GOD. EITHER END YOUR LIFE WHILE
PRAYING, SECONDS BEFORE THE TARGET, OR MAKE
YOUR LAST WORDS: 'THERE IS NO GOD BUT GOD,
MUHAMMAD IS HIS MESSENGER'.

AFTERWARDS, WE WILL ALL MEET IN THE HIGHEST
HEAVEN, GOD WILLING.

IF YOU SEE THE ENEMY AS STRONG, REMEMBER THE
GROUPS [THAT HAD FORMED A COALITION TO FIGHT
THE PROPHET MUHAMMAD]. THEY WERE 10,000.
REMEMBER HOW GOD GAVE VICTORY TO HIS
FAITHFUL SERVANTS. HE SAID: 'WHEN THE FAITHFUL
SAW THE GROUPS, THEY SAID, THIS IS WHAT GOD
AND THE PROPHET PROMISED, THEY SAID THE
TRUTH. IT ONLY INCREASED THEIR FAITH.'

AND MAY THE PEACE OF GOD BE UPON THE
PROPHET.

Glossary of Terms and Definitions

Abu Nidal Organization (ANO): Islamic radical terrorist group also known as Fatah Revolutionary Council or Black September led by Sabri al-Banna. It split from the PLO in 1974. ANO has carried out terrorist attacks in over 20 countries and killed or injured approximately 900 people.

Allah: God. The prophet of Islam, Mohammed, received the Quran which is the word of God/Allah in Arabic.

Al-Gama'a al-Islamiyya: Islamic Group (IG) is led by its spiritual leader, Sheikh Omar Mohammad Abdel Rahman, who is incarcerated in the United States for his role in the conspiracy of the 1993 World Trade Center bombing in New York City.

Al-Qaeda: "The base." The Arabic name given to Osama bin Laden's network of Sunni Muslim Jihad groups that fought in Afghanistan against the Soviet invasion in the late 1980s. Its purpose after the Afghanistan-Soviet war is to overthrow non-Islamic regimes and expel Westerners from Muslim countries. Their goals and determination was explicitly shown on September 11, 2001, when they attacked the United States.

Al-Qaeda Manual: The training manual developed by operatives of al-Qaeda and used as a procedural guide for

Islamic Terrorists. It includes procedures on weapons, secret codes, counter-surveillance, assassinations, disguises, explosives and more.

Ammonium Nitrate and Fuel Oil (ANFO): An explosive material used in the Oklahoma City bombing by Timothy McVeigh in 1995.

Armed Islamic Group (GIA): Radical Islamic terrorist group based out of Algeria created to fight the secular government. The GIA has attacked numerous civilian targets and is responsible for the thwarted plan to bomb the Los Angeles International Airport on December 31, 1999.

Aryan Nations: A white supremacist, neo-nazi, separatist group advocating a separate white nation known to become violent against minorities and government officials.

Aum Shinrikyo: Meaning the Supreme Truth in Japanese. The Aum Shinrikyo Cult was created by Shoko Asahara, in 1987, in Japan. It is a radical religious cult responsible for the deadly Sarin nerve gas attacks on several Tokyo subway trains in 1995.

Blasting Caps: Explosive devices used to set off a charge and detonate an explosive/bomb.

Branch Davidians: A sect of the Seventh-Day Adventists movement. Theologically, the various Davidian groups, of which Branch Davidians is best known, are considered cults of Christianity. Mentioned in this book is the faction, based in Waco, Texas, led by David Koresch which launched an armed resistance to federal agents which ended in an assault by federal agents and a deadly fire set by Koresch on April 19, 1993.

Cleric: Meaning an individual of the clergy or religious inclination.

Collateral Damage: Casualties or damages outside of the intended target of a military or terrorist attack.

CTR (Currency Transaction Report): Money transactions throughout, into, and out of the United States, require the filing of a CTR when those transactions meet or exceed ten thousand dollars.

Deconfliction: A procedure to avoid conflicting investigations or law enforcement efforts to avoid injuries to officers or hindering investigations.

Detonation Cord: A flexible cord containing a center core of high explosives used to detonate other explosives.

Drop Address: An address used for mailing property acquired through the use of fraudulent means or theft, such as the use of a stolen credit card, that cannot be connected to the perpetrator.

EBT: Electronic Benefit Transfer. An EBT is issued in the form of a card by a state or the US Department of Agriculture instead of issuing food stamps or money as a social service /welfare benefit.

Edward P. Murrah Building: The federal building in Oklahoma City bombed by Timothy McVeigh on April 19, 1995.

En Nahda: An Islamic radical terrorist organization founded in Tunisia that imparts their beliefs that an Islamic society must exist throughout the world.

Extremists: Persons or a group with extremely radical doctrine to the point of anti-social behavior, violence or harassment.

Fatwa: A religious ruling in Islam.

Hamas: The Islamic Resistance Movement. It was formed in 1987 as a Palestinian branch of the Muslim Brotherhood. Hamas is responsible for numerous suicide bombings against Israeli targets.

Hawala: The system of transferring money in and out of a country based on trust awhile no money changes hands between remitters. Hawalas were used to bring illegal funds to terrorists in the US.

Hashisheen: The term used to describe a person in Islamic extremism who is heavily partaking in smoking hash just prior to a suicide mission. Often, the hashisheen does this to develop the courage to carry out the mission.

Hizballah: The Party of God. It is also known as Islamic Jihad. It is an Islamic Radical group formed in Lebanon opposing Israel and Middle-East peace negotiations. It is extremely anti-Western and is responsible for numerous terrorist attacks on US interests.

Hizba Tahrir: Also known as the Islamic Liberation Party, Hizba Tahrir is an Islamic radical terrorist organization active in the United States with an extremely anti-United States/anti-Israel ideology.

Identity Theft: A crime in which someone's identity information (date of birth, social security number, etc...) is stolen for the purpose of creating illegal profits and new identities. Credit cards, bank accounts and checks are often redirected to the criminal who makes money from illegal transactions. Identity Theft is increasingly popular and lucrative for terrorists active within the United States and victimizing US citizens.

Ideology: Belief or doctrine.

Islamic Radicals: Followers of Islam with radical beliefs that manifest themselves through terrorism.

Jew York: A derogatory name for New York City created and used by racists, anti-Semites, and terrorists who claim that New York is home to numerous people of the Jewish faith. These racists, anti-Semites and terrorists blame Jews for all the worlds' problems.

Jihad: Meaning struggle within the religion of Islam, Jihad is used by Islamic radicals/terrorists to refer to a holy war and justify their use of violence and destruction to force Islam on non-Islamic societies.

Knock and Talk: A tactic used by police to knock on a person's door to gather information about a certain subject. It is also used to visit the homes of suspected criminals to develop further information.

Middle Eastern Organized Crime (MEOC): Organized criminal groups mostly consisting of criminals of Middle Eastern descent.

Muslim: A person of Islamic faith.

Muslim Brotherhood: Officially called Jamiat al-Ikhwan al-Muslimun [Arab., Society of Muslim Brothers], it is a religious and political organization founded (1928) in Egypt by Hasan al-anna. It is opposed to secular tendencies in

Islamic nations. The organization has sought to foster a return to the original precepts of the NK "http://www.encyclopedia.com/html/Q/Quran.asp. It grew rapidly, establishing an educational, economic, military, and political infrastructure. Threatened by its power, Egypt's government twice banned (1948, 1954) the organization. It has since existed largely as a clandestine but militant group, marked by its rejection of Western influence.

Osama bin Laden: Born in Saudi Arabia to a Yemeni family, bin Laden left Saudi Arabia in 1979 to fight against the Soviet invasion of Afghanistan. As an icon in the Soviet-Afghan war, bin Laden gained many followers. As a result, he trained terrorists and created a global terrorist network called al-Qaeda. Bin Laden and al-Qaeda is responsible for attacks such as the 1993 World Trade Center bombing, the attacks on US Embassies overseas, the USS Cole and the September 11, 2001 attacks.

Plastic Explosives: Explosive substance.

Purification Process: The process of purifying one's body before conducting a suicide mission. The suicide operative may shave the external or all body hair, use Middle Eastern oils and perfumes and pray to Allah..

Randy Weaver Family: A family headed by Randy Weaver that was the subject of a raid by federal agents stemming from possession and sale of illegal weapons charges. They are self-proclaimed white separatists.

Semtex: An explosive substance.

Synergy: The result of a coordination of effort creating a greater success than when individual efforts are deployed.

Terrorcrats: A term used by extremist groups and anti-American groups to refer to the US Government, their officials, law enforcement officers and corporate leaders.

Washitaw Nation: An African-American group with Sovereign citizen ideology that believes America's laws do not apply to them.

Weapons of Mass Destruction (WMD): Weapons of Mass Destruction include chemical, biological and nuclear weapons.

ZOG: Zionist Occupied Government. Zionist refers to people of Jewish faith.

**Also provided by
CTS Associates Incorporated:**

PRODUCTS

The Pocketguide Series published by Looseleaf Law

SERVICES

Protective Services
Private Investigation

TRAINING COURSES

Basic Gang Identification Course
Gang Interdiction Course (LEO)
Street Smarts: A Crime Prevention Course
Interview and Interrogation
Hostage Negotiation Course
Dignitary and Executive Protection Course
Language Immersion Courses

…plus many more courses available

UPCOMING SEMINARS

Dealing with Gangs Effectively: The Seminar
Terrorism: *The threat in the US*

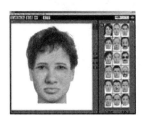 
116

> *The liberties of our country,*
> *the freedom of our civil constitution,*
> *are worth defending against all*
> *hazards; it is our duty to*
> *defend them against all attacks.*

Samuel Adams